Natalie the Great Babysitter
Adventures with Alex and Timmy

Noah's Ark

Volume 2

Annie Hendren

ISBN 979-8-89130-988-3 (paperback)
ISBN 979-8-89243-079-1 (hardcover)
ISBN 979-8-89130-989-0 (digital)

Christian Faith Publishing
832 Park Avenue
Meadville, PA 16335
www.christianfaithpublishing.com

Printed in the United States of America

Natalie the Great Babysitter
Adventures with Alex and Timmy

Noah's Ark
Volume 2

Annie Hendren

Mr. Roberts was waiting outside for Alex to come home from school. He looked down the street and saw Alex walking with Timmy and Natalie. "Hello, kids! How was school today?"

"It was great, Mr. Roberts," Natalie and Timmy said.

"I had a great day, Dad," Alex said. Alex looked at his dad and asked how his day was. Mr. Roberts looked at Alex and said, "I had a great day also. Natalie, are you free Saturday night to watch Alex?"

"I am free," she replied.

"How does 4:00 p.m. sound?"

"See you then, Alex," Natalie said.

It was late Saturday afternoon, and Timmy and Alex were just finishing a snack. Timmy asked his mom, "I think Alex and I are finished with our snack. Is it okay if we work on my model?"

Timmy's mom said, "Please put your dishes in the dishwasher and go wash your hands."

"Thanks, Mom," Timmy said.

GLUE
MARK
GLUE
STICK
MARK

"Timmy and Alex went downstairs. I want you to see a model I am building," Timmy said.

"I love building models," Alex said. "This is cool!"

"I am building Noah's ark," Timmy said.

"Can I help you with it?" asked Alex.

"Yes, I was hoping you would say that," Timmy said.

GLUE
MARK
GLUE
STICK

Natalie walked into the room and asked, "What are you, guys, doing?"

Timmy replied, "We are working on my model of Noah's ark."

"I love the story of Noah's ark," Natalie said. "Do you guys want to hear the story?"

Both Timmy and Alex said yes! Natalie began her story while they were putting the model together.

GLUE
MARK
GLUE
STICK

"Noah was a very wonderful man and a close friend of God's," Natalie began.

"Wow, I would like to be a close friend of God's!" Timmy exclaimed.

Natalie said, "You know we can talk to God any time. God is always around us. God hears every little prayer and knows everything that is going on with us."

"My dad said that God is very busy watching over all of us," Alex said.

Natalie continued telling her story. "God became very sad and angry with the dishonest behavior and violence that was occurring on earth."

Timmy said, "My dad and mom always taught us never to lie, cheat, or steal."

"My dad said you should always try to help people around you if they need it," Alex added.

"Sometimes it's hard to see if someone is in need. A simple smile and 'How are you today?' may be just what another person needs," Natalie said.

Timmy and Alex agreed.

"God said, 'Noah my friend, I have found a way to clean the earth. I want you to build an ark. I need it to be big enough to hold every species of animal, one set, male and female. Make a lower, second, and third deck. There will be enough room for your wife, your three sons, and their wives,'" said Natalie.

Alex asked, "Every kind of animal on earth, male and female?" Timmy looked at Alex and Natalie. "That's a big boat!"

"Noah and his sons worked hard building this beautiful ark for God. They then collected all the supplies that they would need for all the animals and for the family. Think about the amount of grain, hay, and freshwater they had to collect just for the animals," Natalie said.

Timmy said, "That is a lot."

"Remember, they also had to store all the supplies on the ark. That must have been a big boat," Alex said. "Natalie, do you know how big the ark was?"

"It was approximately 450 feet long, 80 feet wide, and 50 feet high."

"Wow! That's a big boat," Alex replied.

"The skies were turning gray. Noah and his sons gathered all the animals, two by two, male and female. They started loading the ark with the passengers."

"That must have been so hard to capture and then load the animals into the ark," Timmy said.

Natalie and Alex agreed!

"Then God told Noah, 'Go into the ark with your family and the animals.' God shut them into the ark. 'In seven days, I will send rain.' God sent rain for forty days and forty nights. The family watched the rain through the windows of the ark. There was so much rain!" Natalie said.

"At the end of forty days and forty nights, Noah opened a window and sent a raven out, and the raven came back. Noah waited for another seven days and sent a dove out. It came back with an olive leaf. Noah waited for another seven days and sent out another dove, and the dove did not return."

"I wonder what happened to the Dove," Timmy said.

"It found dry land," Natalie said.

"God created a gust of wind, and the waters started to dry."

"Wow, imagine having enough power to create wind," Alex said.

"Try to blow air out of your mouth, not a lot comes out," Timmy said.

Natalie continued with her story. "God told Noah it was now safe to leave the ark. Noah and his family started unloading the animals. All the animals left the two by two from the ark."

Natalie said, "This is my most favorite part of this story. God told Noah He had thought of a very special agreement between Himself and every man, woman, child, and living creature for all future generations."

Alex looked at Natalie and asked, "What could that be?"

Natalie said, "Every time you see a rainbow, it will remind all of us of our special bond and the ability to speak with God!"

Timmy said, "I am going to share this story during the show and tell on Monday at school!"

GLUE
GLUE STICK

Natalie looked at the boys and said, "Please make sure you are always kind and good to others!"

"That was a great story!" Alex said.

"It is one of my favorite stories," Timmy said. "Thanks, Natalie, for sharing that with us!"

God bless our beautiful world and every man, woman, child, and living creature!

The end

About the Author

Annie Hendren has always held close to her soul that truth begets good and blossoms into light! Annie spent the first part of her life raising two talented, caring, and contributing children, along with many wonderful dogs and an amazing husband.